Table of Cont

FOREWORD

I Am a Butterfly

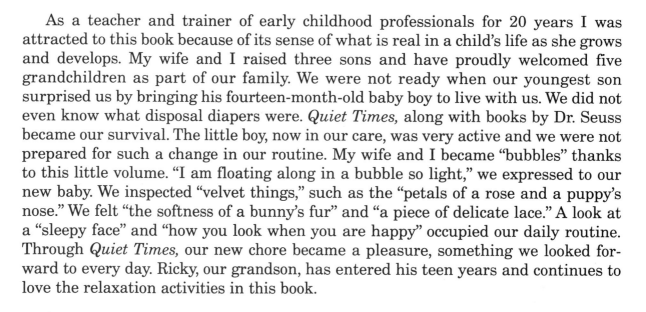

"I am a butterfly, up in the sky. The winds blow me softly, to left and to right." What better way to relax than to visualize yourself as a butterfly. Louise Binder Scott has packed this succinct volume with loads of relaxation activities which have proven to be a forecast of what scientists are now telling us about how the brain develops. Devices for relaxation such as breathing activities, body control, exercises that project feelings, and attention to the senses all contribute to brain development in young children.

As a teacher and trainer of early childhood professionals for 20 years I was attracted to this book because of its sense of what is real in a child's life as she grows and develops. My wife and I raised three sons and have proudly welcomed five grandchildren as part of our family. We were not ready when our youngest son surprised us by bringing his fourteen-month-old baby boy to live with us. We did not even know what disposal diapers were. *Quiet Times,* along with books by Dr. Seuss became our survival. The little boy, now in our care, was very active and we were not prepared for such a change in our routine. My wife and I became "bubbles" thanks to this little volume. "I am floating along in a bubble so light," we expressed to our new baby. We inspected "velvet things," such as the "petals of a rose and a puppy's nose." We felt "the softness of a bunny's fur" and "a piece of delicate lace." A look at a "sleepy face" and "how you look when you are happy" occupied our daily routine. Through *Quiet Times,* our new chore became a pleasure, something we looked forward to every day. Ricky, our grandson, has entered his teen years and continues to love the relaxation activities in this book.

Think about what the title *Quiet Times* invokes in your memories. Can you remember when you were a child? We all have a little child in us somewhere deep down inside. Can you recall those soft and simpler times of rest and coziness you felt as a baby? Curling up in your mother's lap as she read books about bears and beanstalks, poodles and petunias, possums and peacocks that gave you a sense of belonging. You were the focus of something that created an imagination which was soon to grow and express itself through music, literature, and art. It was the sublime experience of nurturing that evolved into an appreciation of the environment and an understanding of those things that contribute to well-being.

What scientists are telling us today is that those early experiences of nurturing, and cultivating natural images in the child, are precursors of brain development. The brain records, decodes, communicates, and stores feelings of security and love in a vast network of connections called "synapses." The synapses or connections among brain cells (neurons) are pathways in the brain to be called upon in future experiences, when the need arises. Touching, the feeling of closeness, relaxation, visualization, and contact with the senses creates wiring in the brain. For many years, neuroscientists assumed that genetics were alone responsible for what an adult was to become. They did not give much attention to nurturing as a device for building adult character. The argument was known as the *nature vs. nurture* conflict.

What scientists can see through electronically scanning the brain is the firing in a synaptic gap as an axon of one brain cell connects with the dendrites of other brain cells or "neurons." This connection is both electrical and chemical. Many neuro-transmitter chemicals, such as serotonin and dopamine, contribute to a profuse firing of these synapses. One axon in a child's brain can contribute to a profuse firing of these synapses as it contacts possibly 15,000 dendrites in milliseconds—the same as driving a car 450 miles (724 km) per hour. If the brain's wiring were laid out lengthwise like a telephone line, it would stretch approximately 600 miles (965 km). If spread out flat, the wiring in a three-year-old's brain would cover the top of a kitchen table. Although this is a very graphic explanation, the implication of the brain studies is very simple. Something Louise Binder Scott knew, many years before the scientists came up with their sophisticated theories, was that when you hold a baby, sing to a toddler, read a poem to a three-year-old, and dance with a four-year-old child, something "magic" happens. Now we know what this "magic" is. One brain cell tells 15,000 other brain cells that these are fun experiences. These neurons which are contacted store this information away for future reference. This explains the phrase "wiring the brain." When this nurturing is not continued and reinforced by activities such as those found in *Quiet Times,* the synapse that first recorded the happening will be pruned from the brain and never be used again. This experience will be lost forever. To illustrate further, when you use the activities given in *Quiet Times* about feelings, such as "What Do Feelings Look Like?" you ask the children to imagine they are happy, sad, sleepy, and mad. By structuring learning opportunities about feelings, along with opportunities to think about "velvet things" and the difference between quiet and noisy, the teacher is preparing "brain food" for young learners. Their neurons are communicating with one another at a rate of 15,000 at one time—an awesome number of instant connections.

If you leave a baby in the crib, never hold her, and seldom say endearing baby talk to the infant, the brain cells (neurons) start to mistrust the signals they are receiving and they atrophy, die, and are lost forever. Neglect and abuse create havoc in the brain like electrical lines and poles which topple in a severe storm. Talking to a baby, doing relaxation activities with a toddler, reading picture books with a young learner, and practicing quiet times techniques can repair the brain damage and build new and stronger neural pathways.

Get in the Flow

Daniel Goleman in his best seller *Emotional Intelligence: Why It Can Matter More than IQ* (Bantam Books, 1995), recommends an idea called the *flow* as a new model for the education of young children. Goleman explains the experience as "a glorious one: the hallmark of the flow is a feeling of spontaneous joy, even rapture. Because the flow feels so good, it is intrinsically rewarding. It is a state in which people become utterly absorbed in what they are doing, paying undivided attention to the task, their awareness merged with their actions." He illustrates that the "flow" is experienced by a surgeon in the midst of a critical operation and is seen in an athlete excelling in a sporting event. The "flow" can be seen in the faces of children as they listen to "The Ho-Hum Story" in *Quiet Times*. Total concentration is evoked when "projected relaxation" is being practiced by young children.

"Howard Gardner, the Harvard psychologist who developed the theory of multiple intelligences, sees flow and the positive states that typify it, as part of the healthiest way to teach children, motivating them from inside rather than by threat or promise of reward." Gardner's theory revolves around natural competencies, according to Goleman. "A child who is naturally talented in music or movement, for example will enter flow more early in that domain than in those where she is less able." Gardner and Goleman both stress the importance of "channeling emotions toward a productive end."

From the time a baby opens its eyes for the first time and looks upon a parent the child begins the journey of creating pathways in the brain. No two persons have the same number of neurons at birth and throughout their lives. Approximately 100 billion brain cells are available to the newborn to make connections that will last a lifetime. Goleman's theory of the flow begins immediately. What the newborn will become, as an adult, will depend on two major factors: what the baby brings as a genetic matrix and how the nurturing environment contributes to the child's development.

Multiple Intelligences

Gardner's theory has seven major intelligences: verbal/linguistic, logical/mathematical, visual/spatial, bodily/kinesthetic, musical/rhythmic, interpersonal, and intrapersonal. Two additional intelligences have been developed and more are sure to be added. The two new intelligences are natural and transcendental. Gardner suggests that we use the child's positive states to draw her/him into learning in the domains where she/he can develop competencies. "You learn at best when you have something you care about and you can get pleasure from being engaged in" (*Frames of Mind*, Basic Books, 1993).

Quiet Times offers children and caregivers an opportunity to practice learned relaxation. When children learn to relax they not only learn to reduce stress, but they also slow down so they can get into the flow of learning as illustrated by Goleman. Many times children are told to "Be QUIET!" by adults as a way of commanding their silence and curtailing their behavior. Instead of this directive, children need opportunities to learn the importance of their quiet times.

It has been approximately 15 years since scientists have turned from the "nature vs. nurture" argument to the philosophy that nurture assists nature in child development. The current theory now supports what Louise Binder Scott and others have been teaching for decades: "All children benefit from periods of rest and feelings of serenity during the day. Many children need to learn how to feel quiet, and if they are to do this, some definite structured periods of relaxation are necessary. It should be one of the objectives of every teacher to provide these periods."

Quiet Times has been a blessing to our family. I know it will add to your classroom by providing the flow in your lesson plans. This volume will wire the children's brains with "I Am a Robot," "The Tired Caterpillar," "Counting Daisies," "This Brown Hen," "Floppy Freddie," and many, many more delightful relaxation activities.

What a blessing it is to be able to think of something quiet!

Quiet Times and Multiple Intelligences

Perhaps, this is the time to take a brief look at how well Louise Binder Scott's approach to relaxation and serenity fits with Howard Gardner's theory of multiple intelligences. A child who exhibits interpersonal skills is one who makes and maintains friends easily, understands and respects others, is a leader, can resolve conflicts, and likes to be with others. Teachers can recognize these attributes as they watch children play. The section "Action Rhymes for Relaxation" in this text lends itself to finding those children who work well with others. Also, when action rhymes are used children with bodily/kinesthetic intelligences can excel. Children with this intelligence are "body smart." They tend to be highly coordinated, use gestures and body language, love role-playing, and enjoy dancing and swaying. A child who has musical intelligence will have a good sense of rhythm and melody, likes to sing, enjoys listening to music, and enjoys creating music. In certain situations different intelligences are called upon to become dominate. A child who works within her chosen intelligence will learn more rapidly and enjoy the experience. A child who is forced into an intelligence she feels is either not fun or is threatening to the individual will rebel and have learning trauma.

The value of the section "Stories for Relaxation" is that it is built on nature stories with quiet, and even sleepy, settings. An environment unfamiliar to many urban children, "The Sleepy Farm," "The Dream Fence," and "The Shadowy, Shady Tree" bring nature into the classroom through imagination and visualization. The activities within this section are obviously rewarding to children with intrapersonal intelligence. These children need time to process information; they think about their own thinking, they know themselves well and like quiet time alone. People who are "nature smart" are aware of their natural surroundings; they like flowers and trees and animals. Pets and farms are part of their dreams. Those children who have natural intelligence might choose careers as ecologists or oceanographers.

Logical/mathematical and linguistic intelligences are fostered by curricula of choice in most preschool through twelfth grade schools in the United States. Logical/mathematical children think in numbers, use abstract symbols well, and are good in math. Word smart, or linguistically talented students, learn through reading, writing, and discussing. They spell easily and think in words. Again, "Action Rhymes for Relaxation" foster both logical and linguistic talents in young children.

Musical and spatial intelligences, in Gardner's theory, seem to be the most evasive to teachers who have been trained in methods classes to be logical/mathematical and linguistic. Here, the section "Devices for Relaxation" steps forward to present "Magic Things," "Music for Relaxation," and "Things to Imagine." Children who are art/space smart think in pictures, learn through visuals, and like to draw and create.

Many famous people have exhibited their dominate intelligence by choice of profession and excelling in their performance. A few of these people are:

- Linguistic—William Shakespeare, John Steinbeck, Emily Dickinson, Jane Austin, Henry David Thoreau

- Logical/Mathematical—Albert Einstein, Bertrand Russell, Marie Curie, Isaac Newton, Bill Gates

- Bodily/Kinesthetic—Mary Lou Retton, Michael Jordan, Babe Ruth, Monica Seles, Martha Graham

- Natural—Charles Darwin, Carl Sagan, Jane Goodall, Jacques-Yves Cousteau

- Art/Spatial—Georgia O'Keeffe, Pablo Picasso, Claude Monet, Fredric Remington

- Musical—Ludwig van Beethoven, Madonna, Louis Armstrong, Wolfgang Amadeus Mozart, Duke Ellington

The Benefits of *Quiet Times*

For some children, serenity is an acquired skill. For others who may be intrapersonal, quiet time is a part of their genetic and environmental heritage. Structured relaxation in *Quiet Times* is designed to create new and varied transition activities for a classroom that has an already busy curriculum. Activities presented here can decrease disruptive behavior, increase attention span, develop a satisfying self-image, and help to control anxiety in students. Children with difficulties in adjusting to the classroom environment, because they have oral communication problems or emotional disorders, can especially benefit from this text. Relaxation activities are fun. Children should look forward to their quiet periods.

There are four sections in *Quiet Times*:

Stories for Relaxation

This section concentrates on natural intelligences. The activities employ images of nature, where the child becomes involved in a natural scene. Pleasant experiences here involve feelings of repose, softness, and dream time. Children of all ages can call upon these early experiences at any stage in their lives. Adults can recognize repose if they were exposed to these techniques when they were very young. It is more difficult for an adult to learn to visualize and relax than for a child who has leaned these techniques naturally. The stories for relaxation offered in *Quiet Times* are designed for preschool, kindergarten, and first grade students, but the materials can be used effectively in all grades including adult education classes.

Devices for Relaxation

The use of mental images can produce sharp drops in muscular tension and a reduction of blood pressure. This section includes: "Using Images," "Projected Relaxation," "Breathing Activities," "Body Control Activities," "Activities for Feelings," and "Using the Senses." The design of mental imaging is to use the activity that is appropriate to the occasion. Unlike most curricula, the purpose for these activities is almost serendipitous. The exercises can fit anywhere in the lesson plan and should not be restricted to a particular time of day. It is suggested that the teacher begin and end each day with one of these selections, but this does not mean it is written into the curriculum to be done at a certain hour. The lesson plan should lead children into their quiet times as individuals as well as collectively.

Bodily/kinesthetic intelligences are represented in this section as well as inter-personal, logical/mathematical, and linguistic emphasis. Research shows that when children learn these techniques early in life, they become better and more productive students in later school years.

Action Rhymes for Relaxation

This section uses spatial and logical/mathematical intelligences as well as bodily/kinesthetic activities. Movement can activate the imagination, help to express a mood, and release creative energy. Children can use their interpersonal intelligences by cooperating in a group activity.

Children love to pretend. With activities from *Quiet Times*, they can become a teddy bear, a robot, a sunflower, and a caterpillar. They can count the daisies as they experience new things about their bodies: how they move and turn, gesture, and manipulate their muscles.

Quiet Poems

Finally, we transition to a time everyone enjoys. The teacher reads these poems as the children sit or lie in relaxed positions. We need to learn to listen as a part of our intrapersonal intelligence. There is a time when children are ripe for the acquisition of listening skills. Each child has his/her own biological clock. A creative teacher can recognize when that clock is ticking and when it sounds an alarm. Many times that clock is wound too tightly and needs some special care to unwind. The quiet times give children time to reflect, evaluate, plan, and create in their minds. How pleasant it is to learn to relax and enjoy nature at an early age. When we find the child in ourselves, we can relax by allowing our anxieties and fears to dissipate and remember a time with Louise Binder Scott's words "Just nothing in this whole wide world, but sky, trees, cloud, and ME!"

by JIM POWELL, ED.D.

INTRODUCTION

The Value of Relaxation

Children as well as adults can suffer from stress. All children benefit from periods of rest and feelings of serenity during the day. Many children need to learn how to feel quiet, and if they are to do this, some definite structured periods of relaxation are necessary. It should be one of the objectives of every teacher to provide these periods.

Among the benefits to be gained from using structured relaxation techniques are a decrease in disruptive and aggressive behavior, an increased attention span, a satisfying self-image, and control of anxiety and tension (especially for children with oral communication difficulties or emotional problems). These relaxation activities should be fun, and the children should look forward to their quiet periods. Frequent sessions of enjoyable relaxation will pay dividends for both teacher and children.

The Activities in *Quiet Times*

Quiet Times provides **planned relaxation activities** which help children:

- Feel a sense of quiet and release from tension.
- Contrast tension and relaxation.
- Develop sense perception and awareness of the beauty around them.
- Create a satisfying self-concept, poise, and confidence.

The book contains four sections: "Stories for Relaxation," "Devices for Relaxation," "Action Rhymes for Relaxation," and "Quiet Poems." Although the activities are designed for preschool, kindergarten, and first grade, many of the selections, particularly the "Devices for Relaxation," can be used effectively with second or third graders, or even older children in a group or clinical situation. These materials have been tested with primary children satisfactorily and are effective whether used by small or large groups of children.

Many of the activities employ images. Research by psychologists has shown that considerable relaxation can be achieved by the use of images. Nature images, where the child can feel a part of a pleasant scene, can produce sharp drops in muscular tension. This is combined with projected relaxation, where the teacher suggests that the children relax or tighten certain parts of the body.

There are additional educational benefits that can be gained by using the rhymes and stories in *Quiet Times*. These activities can help to:

- Improve speech and language.

- Instill social consciousness. (Children learn to cooperate and share with others, build better relationships, and establish positive attitudes toward learning.)

- Teach children to think in orderly fashion. (Rhythm creates orderliness and helps children think sequentially.)

- Coordinate muscles, acquire body control, and extend the range of movements. (All children enjoy bodily rhythm, especially when accompanied by rhyme.)

Suggestions for Using *Quiet Times*

- Give the relaxation period a title that suggests stillness, such as "Our Quiet Time."

- Sit on a cushion, low stool, or chair so the children will not need to raise their heads to achieve eye contact.

- Allow sufficient time for all children to assemble and seat themselves on a rug or on individual mats by giving a "resting signal," such as playing a few notes on an autoharp or piano, or playing a selected piece of music on CD or audio cassette.

- Begin with a short poem or exercise (such as the one below) before reading a story. Do each exercise with the class.

> This is my quiet time.
> My lips are closed,
> My face is still,
> My arms, hands, and feet are still.
> This is my quiet time.

- As you read each story or rhyme, or present an exercise, speak slowly. Use frequent pauses so that children can form images and hold onto them.

- Let your eyes wander occasionally over the group and make a mental note of children who are "wigglers" and appear to be uncomfortable or tense. Those children may benefit from sitting closer to you.

- The mood or climate is important. Relaxation techniques will be more effective if the teacher appears to be relaxed. Children will respond more readily if teachers examine their own states of tension.

STORIES FOR RELAXATION

These stories are designed to induce relaxation and calm feelings. They can be used to follow a concentrated learning activity in which movements have been restricted, or after an intense physical activity in which children have become overstimulated. When children hear a quiet voice or soft music, they will almost automatically tip-toe to their seats. The rhyming quality of the verses in the stories will invite children to participate as the teacher reads.

The Sleepy Farm

Once there was a pleasant little farm. It had a neat white house with shutters. It had a friendly barn. It had fields of sweet-smelling clover where bees buzzed a drowsy tune on almost any warm afternoon.

It was a grazy day, a hazy day; *(Children repeat verses with teacher.)*
A sleepy, slumbery, lazy day.
A fine day for just buzzing around
A day peaceful with sound.

The farm made you feel all quiet inside, because—because it was, shh . . . a sleepy farm. Shh . . . *(Children imitate the sound.)*
On that sleepy farm lived a little yellow chicken. "Cheep, cheep, cheep!" peeped the little yellow chicken. "I think it must be time."

So she snuggled down in her mother's nest, *(Children repeat verses quietly.)*
And under soft feathers she had a good rest.

On that sleepy farm lived a fuzzy baby duckling. "Quack, quack, quack," quacked the fuzzy baby duckling. "I guess it's time. Quack!"

So she found some leaves that she used for a bed, *(Children repeat verses.)*
And under her wing she tucked her head.

On that sleepy farm lived a playful brown puppy with long ears. "Ruff, ruff, ruff," barked the playful brown puppy with long ears. "I have played very hard, but now I can rest for a while."

So he stretched and he stretched in the noonday sun. *(Children slowly stretch and repeat verses.)*
He was much too tired to jump and run.

On that sleepy farm lived a little spotted pig with a curly tail. "Oink, oink, oink," grunted the little spotted pig with a curly tail. "This is the part of the day I like best. Ho-hum! I must be going."

So he found a mud puddle, all cozy and warm, *(Children fold arms over chests and repeat verses.)*
And he wallowed and slept on that sleepy farm.

On that sleepy farm lived a little red rooster. He was just learning how to crow. "Er, er, er, er, err!" crowed the little red rooster in a squeaky voice. *(Teacher asks the children to make the rooster sound with him/her.)* He was very, very sleepy.

So he sat on his favorite branch of a tree, *(Children repeat verses.)*
Behind some green leaves where no one could see.

On that sleepy farm lived a little boy. It was the warmest time in the afternoon. The little boy yawned, "Ho-hum," and again he yawned, "Ho-hum." *(Children yawn.)* He tried to keep back the yawns, but he just couldn't. They came out, one after the other.

So he lay on some grass in the nice, cool shade, *(Children lie on rug and repeat verse.)*
And he watched the shapes the fluffy clouds made.

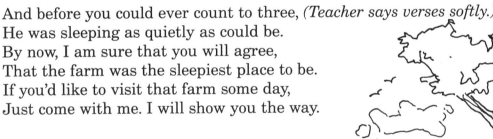

And before you could ever count to three, *(Teacher says verses softly.)*
He was sleeping as quietly as could be.
By now, I am sure that you will agree,
That the farm was the sleepiest place to be.
If you'd like to visit that farm some day,
Just come with me. I will show you the way.

On a grazy day, a hazy day; *(Children repeat verses.)*
A sleepy, slumbery, lazy day.

The Dream Fence

I am sure that you have all heard about Wee Willie Winkie who lives in Mother Goose Land. Let's listen to Wee Willie Winkie's "Dream Fence" story.

Wee Willie Winkie has built a dream fence to separate Wide-Awake Land from Sleepy Land. He has asked Miss Muffet's spider to spin a thin silver web between each fence post. The fence posts all lean lazily over to one side. They do not stand up straight. Can you imagine the leaning-over fence posts? Show how you would lean over.

To see that sleepy dream fence, you will have to close your eyes, for that is how you can see it best.

Wee Willie Winkie's dream fence is covered with moonbeams—as soft as cotton, as soft as down on a baby duckling, as soft as velvet.

Little shadow pictures fall along the side of the dream fence. Those shadow pictures never seem the same, no matter how often you look at them. Sometimes the shadow pictures are white. Sometimes they are gray. And sometimes they are a deep blue, depending upon how big the moon is and how brightly it shines. The moon makes lovely pictures on the dream fence.

If there is a thin sliver of moon, the shadows make tiny silver dots all over the fence. But if the moon is as round as a cookie, the shadows make big splashes on the fence. You never know what to expect and that is why the dream fence always holds such nice surprises.

When you close your eyes, the most wonderful things happen. *(Pause after each image is mentioned.)* You can see soft, fuzzy baby chicks, or cuddly puppies, and sometimes you can see shadows that look like flowers or leaves or dancing butterflies. It is so much fun imagining those shadow pictures, and the more you think about them, the more relaxed your body feels, until you cannot hold up your head any more at all. Ahhhh! *(Sigh.)* Your eyelids feel so heavy and your whole body feels so limp that the only thing you can do is to go to sleep. It makes me sleepy just telling about it, so I know exactly how you must be feeling right now as you listen—all cozy, and warm, and dreamy, and comfortable. I am so sleepy myself that I'm afraid I cannot tell any more just now. Ho-hum! *(Yawn.)*

This story is designed to quiet the children and instill feelings of repose. Read the story softly and slowly, so the children can form vivid mental images of the dream fence. You may wish to duplicate copies of the story to send home for use as a bedtime story, or record it on tape. Read the Mother Goose rhyme "Wee Willie Winkie." Ask one child to be Wee Willie Winkie and touch each member of the group with an imaginary wand, after which the children pretend to go to sleep.

Sleepy Town

Before sharing this story, decide with the children what the names will be for the girl and boy.

Little Black Horse trotted off to Sleepy Town every night. When he left for Sleepy Town, he took a sleepy boy, a sleepy girl, and a sleepy animal with him.

One night Little Black Horse said, "It is time to leave for Sleepy Town and I must get ready." He switched his long tail and he held his head high as he came trotting, trotting, trotting, ever so slowly, with very light hoofbeats. Clippety-clop, clippety-clop. *(Children slap thighs softly with palms. They repeat the trotting refrain slowly each time it occurs in the story.)*

Sally saw him and called,

"Stop, Little Black Horse, Whoa! *(Children repeat with teacher.)*
Stop for me. I want to go."

So Little Black Horse stopped and let Sally climb on his back. Away they went, trotting, trotting, trotting, clippety-clop, clippety-clop, ever so slowly.

Billy called,

"Little Black Horse, please wait for me. *(Children repeat with teacher.)*
I am as sleepy as can be."

Little Black Horse stopped and made a puffing noise with his lips: "Prr!" He shook his mane. Billy climbed on his back and away they went, trotting, trotting, trotting, clippety-clop, clippety-clop, ever so slowly.

Brown Puppy said,

"Woof, woof! If you do not mind, *(Children repeat with teacher.)*
I would like to climb behind."

So Little Black Horse stopped to let Brown Puppy jump on his back and away they went, trotting, trotting, trotting, clippety-clop, clippety-clop, ever so slowly.

Little Black Horse's hoofbeats were as light as clouds and as soft as cotton, over the hilltops, across the meadow to Sleepy Town.

17

"Is it very far?" asked sleepy Sally.

"I can hardly keep my eyes open," said sleepy Billy.

Brown Puppy said, "I have never been so sleepy in my life."

Trotting, trotting, trotting, clippety-clop, clippety-clop.

Little Black Horse came to a gate, *(Children repeat with teacher.)*
Which opened—it was wide.
A gate all made of moonbeams,
And he trotted right inside.

To a meadow with soft grasses,
Where flowers bent their heads,
And little elves lay fast asleep,
On leafy, grassy beds.

A little brook played music,
As it trickled on its way.
A warm breeze sang a lullaby.
This was the place to stay. It was Sleepy Town!

Little Black Horse stopped gently. Sally got off his back. So did Billy. So did Brown Puppy. And Little Black Horse said, "Stay here until morning." However, nobody heard him, for they were all fast asleep.

Then Little Black Horse went trotting, trotting, trotting, clippety-clop, clippety-clop to pick up lots more boys and girls and animals to carry them to Sleepy Town.

Would you like to ride Little Black Horse? You can if you will remember this story at bedtime tonight.

Children can dramatize the story. The characters put their hands on the shoulders of the children in front of them and trot slowly around the room, Little Black Horse leading.

The Ho-Hum Story

Teacher: Once there was a sleepy kitten.
      She said, "Ho-hum. I'm sleepy now,
      So I will curl right up! Meow!" (*Children curl up.*)

Children: (*Children yawn and say verses each time.*) And she did. Ho-hum!
      When cats are sleepy as they can be,
      They yawn and yawn, like you and me. Ho-hum!

Teacher: Once there was a dear little baby lamb.
      He said, "Ho-hum! I must find my mother sheep,
      Then I will go fast asleep." (*Children stretch out and close eyes.*)

Children: And he did. Ho-hum!
      When lambs are sleepy as they can be,
      They yawn and yawn, like you and me. Ho-hum!

Teacher: Once there was a panting puppy.
      She said, "Ho-hum! I chased a cat, and I ran a mile,
      So now I'll have to rest awhile." (*Children sit quietly.*)

Children: And she did. Ho-hum!
      When puppies are sleepy as they can be,
      They yawn and yawn, like you and me. Ho-hum!

Teacher: Once there was a long-eared rabbit.
He said, "Ho-hum! Rabbits play and rabbits hop, *(Children move bodies up and down.)*
But sometimes rabbits have to stop."

Children: And he did. Ho-hum!
When rabbits are sleepy as they can be,
They yawn and yawn, like you and me. Ho-hum!

Teacher: Once there was a newborn brown calf with wobbly legs.
She said, "Ho-hum! Because I was just born today,
I think I'll lie down in this hay." *(Children curl up.)*

Children: And she did. Ho-hum!
When calves are sleepy as they can be,
They yawn and yawn, like you and me. Ho-hum!

Teacher: (Read slowly until voice becomes almost a whisper.) Once there were some children who ran and played and then they were tired. They lay quietly. They closed their eyes. Their mouths opened in big yawns, and soon they were as quiet as snowflakes or flower petals.

If a child should happen to fall asleep, clap hands softly and say:
"Wake up, wake up today,
It is time to work or play."

In the Night

Anna puts on her pajamas and gets into bed. She snuggles down under the warm, friendly quilt.

In the lovely night, Anna hears wind sounds. The wind brushes branches against the window. Swish, swish, swish! *(Children repeat quietly.)* But Anna is not afraid. *(Children repeat.)*

The wind sings a mournful song up and down the scale. "Oo-oo-oo-oo-oo!" *(Children imitate.)* Anna is not afraid. *(Children repeat.)* Anna says, "The wind is singing a lullaby."

Sometimes the rough wind roars and soars and rolls and rattles the doors. It bangs the shutters. But Anna is not afraid. *(Children repeat.)* She knows that the blustery, flustery wind is blowing up rain. It will water the little seeds and help them grow.

Sometimes the thunder goes "Rroom, rroom" like a big bass drum, and the lightning makes a zigzag streak across the sky. But Anna is not afraid. *(Children repeat.)* She knows that thunder and lightning are part of the rainstorm.

The rain comes down— drip, drip, drip, drop, drop, drop. *(Children repeat.)* Soon the rain comes faster and faster—pit, pit, pit, pit, pit. *(Children repeat.)* Anna knows that the dry earth likes rain.

Finally, the rain stops and yellow moonbeams shine through Anna's window. They make a light on the floor. Anna is not afraid. *(Children repeat.)*

Sometimes in the lovely night, Anna hears something run across the floor. Scramble, scramble, scramble! Anna is not afraid. *(Children repeat.)* It is only a tiny mouse looking for a morsel of food.

In the night, Anna hears crickets playing their fiddles: Crick-crick-cree! *(Children repeat.)* Sometimes she hears a humming sound: Mmm! *(Children repeat.)* It's a little mosquito hoping that it might get into Anna's room. Anna is not afraid. *(Children repeat.)*

Sometimes Anna hears, "Hoo-hoo-hoo!" Anna is not afraid. *(Children repeat.)* She knows that a barn owl is flying outside looking for food for her baby owls.

Anna hears footsteps on the stairs: Squeak, squeak, squeak, step, step, step! Anna knows that it is Daddy or Mommy coming upstairs to see that she is all right. Anna is not afraid. *(Children repeat.)*

Anna feels safe, for she knows that the sounds she hears are part of the lovely night. Night is a very nice time. Before you go to sleep, you can think of all the important things you have done that day.

Night is gentle like tiptoeing feet. Night brings shadow pictures on the furniture. Night means a warm quilt that keeps Anna snug and comfortable. Anna sleeps, sleeps, sleeps through the lovely night, because she is not afraid. *(Children repeat.)*

Read this story slowly. It can induce a sense of repose and dispel fear of the dark. Ask: "Have you ever been afraid? Tell about it. What helps you not to be afraid? Is everyone afraid of something?" The character in the story can be changed to a boy.

The Shadowy, Shady Tree

Once there was a sleepy, sleepy place under a shadowy, shady tree. In that sleepy, sleepy place lay a small brown puppy. The puppy stood up. *(Children stand.)* She stretched and yawned, and she stretched and stretched some more. *(Children stretch and yawn.)* Then she went to look for something to nibble and gnaw. She took a bone to her doghouse, but she couldn't keep her eyes open. So she went back to the shadowy, shady tree and went to sleep. *(Children sit down and clasp hands beside head.)*

Once there was a furry, purry, little gray ball of a kitten. He said in a wee, sleepy voice, "Oh, dear! I am so sleepy." So he yawned and yawned and yawned. *(Children yawn.)* He found a basket on the back porch and climbed inside, but he couldn't sleep. So he went to the shadowy, shady tree and under it he curled up like kittens do, and went to sleep. *(Whisper.)*

There was a baby chick who looked for something to eat. The mother hen knew that her baby chick was hungry, so she found some yellow meal for him. She knew that her baby chick was tired, so she led him to the shadowy, shady tree. There she spread out her warm feathers so that he could creep under them. Soon he was asleep. *(Whisper.)*

There was a duckling, quack, quack, quack.
She had soft feathers on her back.
She was tired of swimming and everything,
So she put her head underneath her wing. *(Put arm over head.)*
And there under the shadowy, shady tree,
She slept until it was half past three.

A butterfly, blue, green, and red,
Sat with her wings above her head, *(Raise arms over head and place palms together.)*
On a branch of the shadowy, shady tree,
Oh, what a sleepy place to be!

The children saw all of those marvelous sleepy things. They lay down on their backs under the shadowy, shady tree, just as you are lying now in your very own quiet, sleepy, sleepy place. *(Children lie down.)* And what did they do, boys and girls?

This story can be told in installments. Other animals may be added.

Alexander's Sleepy Time

Puppy said, "I cannot go to sleep until I have said goodnight to Alexander. He gives me bones. He pats my head with his gentle hands. It is sleepy time for dogs and children, but I cannot go to sleep until I have said goodnight to Alexander."

One puppy went into the room, *(Children repeat.)*
Creep, creep, creep, *(Creep fingers.)*
To see if Alexander,
Was asleep, sleep, sleep! *(Fold hands beside head.)*

"I cannot go to bed," said Kitten Cat, "until I have said goodnight to Alexander. He lets me play with a ball of string. He cuddles me in his arms. It is sleepy time for cats and children, but I cannot go to sleep until I have said goodnight to Alexander."

One kitten went into the room, *(Children repeat.)*
Creep, creep, creep,
To see if Alexander,
Was asleep, sleep, sleep!

"I cannot go to sleep," said Baby Bunny, "until I have said goodnight to Alexander. He picks me up carefully and he never pulls my long ears. Sometimes Alexander gives me a sweet carrot. It is sleepy time for bunnies and children, but I cannot go to sleep until I have said goodnight to Alexander."

One bunny went into the room, *(Children repeat.)*
Creep, creep, creep,
To see if Alexander,
Was asleep, sleep, sleep!

And he WAS! Sound asleep!

- Adapted from "Baby Ray" by Eudora Bumstead, **St. Nicholas Magazine,** *1890*

The Seashell

One day at the beach, the wind blew loudly. The waves dashed high on the rocks.

A little seashell from the ocean deep,
Was suddenly awakened from its sleep. *(Children repeat verses quietly.)*

The little seashell was frightened. It cried, "What is happening to me?" Then with one big SWISH, a huge wave tossed the little seashell out on the beach. Everything was still. The wind made a soft whispering sound. The bright sun came out and smiled down upon the trembling little seashell. The wind sang:

"Shh, little seashell lying in the sand.
Do not be afraid. You have friends on the land. Shh!" *(Children repeat.)*

The waves murmured softly:

"Shh, little seashell from the ocean deep.
Listen to my lullaby and soon you'll be asleep." *(Children repeat.)*

Suddenly, the little seashell was picked up and tossed high in the air. A boy just wanted to have some fun, but the little seashell was frightened. And the ocean whispered:

"Shh, little seashell. Just lie very still.
Nothing will bother you. Nothing will. Shh!" *(Children repeat.)*

A tired little girl was crying. She was lost from her mother and father. The little seashell was sorry for the tired little girl. It whispered, "Shh . . . shh . . . shh!" *(Children repeat sound.)*

The tired little girl saw the seashell and she picked it up. "The seashell is talking to me," she said as she stopped crying.

She held the little seashell to her ear to hear the quiet sound: "Shh . . . shh . . . shh!"

Soon the tired little girl's father and mother came along, and they were so happy to see their little girl and know that she was safe. The father picked up his little girl, who was now fast asleep. She still held the seashell and it was pressed close to her ear.

They all went home—the mother, the father, the tired little girl, and the seashell. All night long, the seashell lay on a shelf in the little girl's room and it sang quietly, "Shh . . . shh . . . shh!"

Each time the seashell makes its quiet sound, the children join in saying it. You may want to follow the story with this rhyme:

Little seashell by the sea,
Whisper your quiet sound to me.
"Shh . . . shh . . . shh." *(Children repeat.)*

And I know what I will do!
I'll whisper the sound right back to you.
"Shh . . . shh . . . shh." *(Children repeat.)*

Bring a conch shell or other shells to pass around the group. The children can hold them to their ears and hear the sound of the sea.

The Yawning Puppy

Once there was a puppy who scarcely did anything but sleep and yawn. When he wasn't sleeping, he was yawning. When he wasn't yawning, he was sleeping. Without a doubt, he was the sleepiest puppy in the world.

In the morning, as soon as the sun came up, he would find a tree with spreading branches. Then his mouth would open: "Ow-oop!" (*Children imitate puppy's yawn.*) After that, he would lie down with his hind legs stretched out behind and his front legs stretched out in front, and snooze the morning away.

Sometimes, he would wake up just long enough to find his dish and eat his lunch. Then back he would go to his shady tree, stretch and yawn, "Ow-oop!" and close his eyes for another nap.

In the early evening he was let into the house. He always chose his favorite rug in front of the fireplace, for in winter it was warm and in summer it was cool. He would stretch his legs wide apart behind, and with a bi-i-ig yawn, "Ow-oop," he would place his nose between his two front paws and go to sleep.

It is easy to catch a yawn. It is even more catching than measles. But of course, it is much more pleasant to yawn than to have measles. Everyone who saw the puppy yawning would catch his yawn. He would have everybody yawning long before the sun set behind the red barn.

One evening, Daddy was reading the newspaper. All at once, the puppy opened his mouth wide, showed his white teeth, curled up his long pink tongue, and yawned, "Ow-oop!"

"Awkr-oop!" yawned Daddy, laying down the newspaper. (*Children imitate yawn.*)

Mommy was knitting a sweater for the baby who was coming soon to live with the family. She too, opened her mouth and yawned. "Ho-hum!" (*Children imitate yawn.*)

Granddaddy saw this yawn. His face wrinkled up into what everyone thought would be a laugh, but the laugh did not come. No siree! Out came the biggest, loudest yawn you ever heard, "Ay-y-uh-rk-hum-rup!" (*Children imitate yawn.*)

Grandmother caught Granddaddy's yawn. Her eyes closed for a second. She laid down the book she was reading and raised her hand to shut off the yawn. Too late! Out it came!. "Awk-oh-um!" (*Children imitate yawn.*)

Of course they all went to bed right away.

The same thing happened evening after evening. Everyone was in bed by sundown because of the yawning puppy.

Finally, one evening, just as everyone was beginning to catch the puppy's yawns, Daddy and Mommy decided to do something once and for all. They went out to the toolshed. They measured and hammered and sawed until they had built a doghouse.

"There you are, Puppy," Daddy said. "Mommy and I are giving you a home of your own. Now you can yawn when you feel like it. We cannot keep our eyes open while you are in the house." How do you think the puppy felt about that? (*Pause for responses.*)

The puppy did not seem to mind a bit. The doghouse had a woolly blanket on the floor and a snug warm covering for the door. He was more comfortable than a bug in a rug or a bear in a lair or a chickadee in a cherry tree. There he yawned and slept as much as he pleased.

Then one day, Baby Jon came to live at the house. When he opened his mouth, the biggest sound came out: "Wah! Wah! Wah!"

Daddy sang lullabies to Baby Jon.

Mommy patted Baby Jon.

Granddaddy said, "Goo-goo!" and tried to make Baby Jon laugh.

Grandmother jiggled Baby Jon on her knee.

But Baby Jon kept right on crying, "Wah! Wah! Wah!"

"Dear me, we are getting no sleep at all," sighed the family. They had no time to do their work. There was no time for anything but taking care of wide-awake Baby Jon. However, they could not be angry with Baby Jon, for they loved him so.

Now the yawning puppy grew lonely for his favorite rug in front of the fireplace. He was also quite curious about that strange sound coming from the house. So one evening, he scratched at the door and was let in.

Daddy said, "My! How you have grown!"

Mommy said, "Why, you are a puppy no longer."

The grown-up puppy sniffed at Baby Jon who was being jiggled on Grandmother's knee. Then he opened his mouth, "Ow-oop!"

Baby Jon stopped crying and blinked at the puppy for a long, long time.

"Ow-oop!" This time the yawn was rather gruff and doggy-like.

"Uh," grunted Baby Jon, and before you could say "Tick!" Baby Jon was sound asleep and Granddaddy laid him in his crib.

"Good dog," said Grandmother.

"Good dog," said Granddaddy.

"Good dog," said Daddy.

"Good dog," said Mommy.

Now I suppose you are wondering if the family was able to get their work done. Yes, indeed! Everything was finished right on the dot!

For the yawning puppy was now a big, bounding, bouncing, barking dog, and he yawned only when he was tired from entertaining Baby Jon.

The children imitate all the yawns in the story. Close the story by saying:

Yawn, yawn, yawn, as sleepy as can be.
You, too, will yawn, if you watch and catch the yawns from me.
Yawn, yawn, yawn.

Stimulate conversation by asking, "Do you have a puppy or grown-up dog at home? What is its name? Show how it sleeps. Does your dog know any tricks? How smart is your dog? How do you know it likes you?" Children may dramatize the story and choose characters they wish to play.

Baby Gosling

Baby Gosling was hatched out of an egg that was laid by her mother, Mrs. Goose.

One day, Baby Gosling slipped away from her brothers and sisters. She found a cool blue pond of water. Oh, it was such fun to glide along in the water. Baby Gosling swam and she swam and she swam. *(Children say this line with the teacher each time it is repeated in the story.)*

Baby Gosling was lonesome. She saw a squirrel on the bank of the pond.

"Hello," said Baby Gosling in a very soft voice. "Would you like to play with me?" But the squirrel did not answer, because he was sound asleep.

So Baby Gosling swam and she swam and she swam. Soon she came to a turtle. The turtle was sitting very still.

"Hello," said Baby Gosling. "Would you like to play with me?" But the turtle's head was tucked inside its shell and it was sound asleep.

So Baby Gosling swam and she swam and she swam. Then she saw a rabbit. The rabbit was lying down with its long ears back and it was sound asleep.

There seemed to be no use trying to find someone with whom to play. Baby Gosling swam and she swam and she swam. Soon her swimming became slower and slower and slower until she couldn't swim anymore at all.

She climbed out of the water and found a soft bed of grass and leaves, and she tucked her head under her wing. Soon Baby Gosling was sound asleep like everyone else by the blue sparkling pond. After some searching, that is where Mrs. Goose found Baby Gosling.

Ask: "Did Mrs. Goose awaken her baby or let her sleep? How would a baby duck or gosling sleep? Describe a gosling."

Willie Goes to Bed

Willie was a little boy who never wanted to go to bed.

The clock would say, "Time for bed, Willie."

The bird would say, "Time for bed, Willie," as Father covered its cage.

Mother would say, "It's time for bed, Willie."

But Willie just did NOT want to go to bed.

One evening, Willie whispered to himself, "I'm not going to bed anymore. There must be a better way to sleep and I am going to find it."

So Willie went out to the porch and there was Cat curled up in a round furry ball, sound asleep.

"Cat knows the best way to sleep," said Willie. "That's for me." And so Willie lay down on the porch and curled up in a ball like Cat. But the porch was hard. Willie twisted and turned, trying to get to sleep.

Soon Cat woke up and said, "I've had my catnap. Come on and let's play."

But Willie was grumpy. "Taking a catnap is no way to sleep," he said. "There must be a better way."

"Is that so?" said Cat. "Then let's find out how Rooster sleeps. You may like his way better."

So Cat followed Willie and they went to see how Rooster sleeps. Rooster sat on top of a gate. His head was tucked under his wing.

Willie climbed up on the gate and put his head under his arm. This didn't work. He almost fell off the gate, so he got down in a hurry.

"Sitting on a gate is no way to sleep," said Willie.

"Is that so?" said Cat.

"Is that so?" said Rooster, who was now awake.

"Follow me and I'll show you how to sleep," said Willie.

So Cat and Rooster followed Willie to Willie's house.

"You can't come in," Willie said, "but you can look in the window. Now you will learn the right way to sleep."

Willie went into the bathroom and brushed his teeth and washed his hands and face. He put on his pajamas. He got into bed.

Cat and Rooster sat on the windowsill and watched. By now, Willie was almost asleep.

"What a STRANGE way to sleep," said Cat.

"What a STRANGE way to sleep," said Rooster.

"It's the best . . . way . . . to sleep . . . of . . . all," said Willie as he yawned a big yawn. Meanwhile, Cat and Rooster sat and sat and wondered and wondered why people sleep in such a STRANGE way.

Discuss: "Why did Cat and Rooster think that going to bed was a strange way to sleep? Let's add other characters to the story. Do you think that Willie learned something about sleeping?" Children may dramatize the story and choose characters they wish to play. Encourage comments about the sleeping habits of other animals.

The Black Velvet Kitten

This is a story about a black velvet kitten. My, what a beautiful black velvet kitten she is! She is completely black all over from the top of her head to the tip of her tail. *(Read softly and slowly, with frequent pauses.)*

What do you suppose the black velvet kitten wears around her neck? Well, she wears a black velvet ribbon tied in a bow! It is not a big bow, just a very tiny bow. Some people cannot see the black velvet bow at all, because the black velvet kitten is so very black. The very tiny bow is just a little bit blacker than the black velvet kitten. If you keep looking and looking, you can really see the bow. You can see the two little black velvet loops and the knot in the middle. Black is so lovely.

How that black velvet kitten loves to sleep! And where do you suppose she sleeps? She sleeps in a deep box—a black velvet box. Imagine! The sides of the box inside and out are covered with black velvet. There's also a black velvet cushion at the bottom. That's where the black velvet kitten sleeps. She is sleeping and dreaming. She is dreaming about a place where everything is soft black velvet. How do I know? The black velvet kitten told me.

* * *

Now there is just one way to get to the black velvet country. You must walk down a black velvet sidewalk. Straight ahead. The sidewalk just goes on and on and on as far as you can see. When you step on the black velvet sidewalk, your feet don't make a single sound. It is so soft to walk on. You just keep walking and soon you will come to the black velvet country and by your side will be the black velvet kitten, guiding you every step of the way.

The first thing you see is a lovely fountain named "The Fountain that Drips Water Bells." As each drop of water falls, it takes the shape of a tiny, tiny bell, and it makes a tinkling sound when it falls. There are hundreds of water bells ringing all the time because "The Fountain that Drips Water Bells" never stops. It just goes on forever and ever. The black velvet kitten says that some people sit and watch and listen to the water bells so long that they get sleepy and then they have to come back some other time.

* * *

The little black kitten now takes us into the black velvet house. To enter this house, all you have to do is push the black velvet door open and walk in. It does not make a sound, because its hinges and doorknob are also covered with black velvet.

Inside the black velvet house, there are beautiful black velvet curtains that hang to the floor. You pull open the black velvet curtains slowly, slowly, and you see a black velvet table. On the black velvet table there is a black velvet basket filled with black fruit. It is not black velvet fruit because if it were, we could not eat it. The basket is filled with fruit that has skin on it and is filled with delicious juice. The fruit is shaped like plums, but it doesn't taste like plums at all. It's a lot more delicious. It is called "flums." A flum is the most wonderful, tasty fruit in the whole world, the black velvet kitten says. In the first place, there is no stone in the center of a flum. Only juice—nothing but juice. That juice is so marvelous to taste that it cannot be described. Suppose you take one drop of orange juice, one drop of peach and plum and grape juice, and one drop of juice from every fruit in the whole world, and then add one drop of honey. Well, that is what the juice of a flum tastes like, only it is twice as delicious. You can almost taste the juice now, can't you? *(Pause for responses.)*

There's a funny thing about that basket of flums. There are always forty-one flums in the black velvet basket. No matter how many you eat, there are always forty-one flums. Isn't that amazing? The black velvet kitten says that you might want to stay there and eat five or even fifty flums, but, of course, there are other things to see and do.

*　　*　　*

In order to see what is in another room of that black velvet house, you will have to pull open black velvet curtains. Slowly, slowly, the curtains open. Now you see a beautiful black velvet bed with a big, soft, black velvet pillow, a black velvet pillow as cool and as soft as a cloud. When you lie on the black velvet pillow, a wonderful thing happens! Guess what? *(Pause for responses.)*

As soon as you lay your head back, it sinks down into the pillow, and the whole room is filled with the smell of violets, fresh violets, so lovely and delicate. Just like magic, that black velvet pillow turns into a pillow made of tiny little black violets. Now your head is resting on that sweet-smelling pillow all made of thousands and thousands of violets. Isn't that interesting? Aren't you glad the black velvet kitten found all of these black velvet things? It makes me feel . . . comfortable just thinking about it. Black is so beautiful!

*　　*　　*

Now the black velvet kitten leads us into another room in the black velvet house. Hanging from the ceiling is a big bell that covers the whole ceiling. That bell is covered with . . what do you suppose? *(Pause for responses.)* Yes, black velvet. The outside of the bell is black velvet. The inside of the bell is covered with black velvet and even the clapper is covered with black velvet. I can hardly imagine it, but the black velvet kitten says it is so. When the black velvet bell is rung, it doesn't make the sound a bell usually makes. It makes black velvet music—soft, dreamy music.

All around the edge of the black velvet bell are itty-bitty bells; they are all velvet, too. Now when the big bell is rung, all of the itty-bitty bells ring. There are hundreds of itty-bitty bells and they all play music together. After a long time, the music begins to get fainter and fainter, and soon the music fades away. If you want, you can strike the big black velvet bell and the music will start all over again. It is never the same music, but the music is just as beautiful or even more so. And then the music gets fainter and fainter, and slower and slower, and fades away like mist at the ocean. *(This may be a good time to play a flowing tune on a CD or audio tape player.)*

The black velvet kitten says, "Let's see the wishing well." So we leave the black velvet house and walk to the wishing well. It is a round well and its sides are covered with black velvet. It is not a very wide well, so you could never fall into it. However, you can lean over and look down into it. When you visit that black velvet wishing well, be sure to make a wish because that is the reason the wishing well is there. As you look over into the well, a little blackbird drops one of its feathers into your hand. You hold your hand open and look at the little black feather. It feels so soft. The black velvet kitten says, "You will have to drop the feather into the well," so you drop it. It swirls around and around until you cannot see the black feather anymore at all. And while you are looking, the little blackbird flies along and drops another little black feather into your hand. This one you are supposed to keep, to tuck under your pillow just as you would tuck a tooth that fell out under your pillow and hope the tooth fairy would leave you a dime or a quarter.

"Will my wish come true?" I ask the little black velvet kitten.

"Try it and see," says the black velvet kitten. "It does no harm to believe."

Anyway, boys and girls, tell what your wish would be. I will write down all of your wishes, one at a time. It might take several days to finish all the wishes, but what do you think I will do with the wishes? I will make a book of them, and when you can read the wishes, you will find them most interesting.

— *Adapted; Unable to Trace Author.*

All senses are activated as these stories are read in installments to the children. They "feel" the black velvet, they "taste" the juicy flums, they "hear" the beautiful ringing of the bells, they "smell" the violets, and they "see" the adventures of the black velvet kitten and share them with her.

If a child actually falls asleep during the reading of an episode, clap your hands softly and say:

"Wake up, wake up, it's time to play,
What would you like to do today?"

Children may enjoy making up their own adventures of the black velvet kitten. Bring in swatches of black velvet and pass them around the class. Cut a piece of black velveteen in the shape of a sleeping kitten. Add white crayon features and broomstraws for whiskers. The figure will adhere to a flannel board. Ask, "Which story about the black velvet kitten did you like best? Tell the story."

DEVICES FOR RELAXATION

Using Images

Bubbles. Outside on a sunny morning, make a large pan of soapy water (follow a recipe for soap bubbles) and demonstrate how to blow bubbles with a bubble ring. Ask the children to observe how some bubbles float along, following a path, while other bubbles will burst. Have the children blow bubbles and tell about their experiences. They may draw pictures of rainbow bubbles. Ask the group to describe how it might feel to be blown away like a bubble. Would they feel excited? scared? happy? Then ask them to pretend to be bubbles and move with a floating motion around the room. They may spread their arms to show the size of their bubbles. Say, "Imagine that you are inside a bubble. You are being blown away. Show us how you float. Show us how your bubble might burst. How would you feel inside the bubble? If you were tired of floating, how would you get out of the bubble?"

Ask the children to imagine that the bubble takes them to a new land. Ask: "Would you stay inside the bubble, or would you get out and explore? What kinds of flowers, fruit, and vegetables would you see in the new place? Would you eat any of them? Do you meet anyone? Are the people different from you? How? Do the people speak English or another language? What language?"

Say the following rhyme. Ask the children to perform the actions.

> I am floating along in a bubble so light.
> The gentle breeze blows me away out of sight.
> Quietly go and floating up high, *(Raise arms.)*
> Send my big bubble up to the sky.
> Come back to earth, now we will stop. *("Float" back to rug.)*
> Get out of your bubble by making it pop! *(Clap.)*

Magic Things. Construct play eyeglasses from pipe cleaners. The children will have fun wearing them and imagining "magic things." A child wearing the glasses will feel less self-conscious. This activity will help children observe things they might not see otherwise.

Music for Relaxation. Music for relaxation should be flowing and not rhythmic. Music performed by harps and strings is often soft, soothing music. Select music that is appropriate and have the children listen to it. Follow a listening relaxation activity with a "picturing" session where children draw pictures depicting the scenes they imagined and the feelings they experienced as they heard the music.

When reading the following poem, pause after each line and listen for children's imaginings. At the end, ask the children to name their favorite songs in the quietest voice possible.

Do you know? Do you know?
How to relax from head to toe?
Listen! I will whisper how,
And you will relax yourself right now.
Think of flowers all in bloom.
Smell their very nice perfume.
Think of hills and grass and trees.
Think of buzzing honeybees.
Watch the white clouds float along,
Think about your favorite song.

The Man Without Bones. Once there was a man who had no bones in his neck. He could not hold up his head. *(Bend head to one side.)* The poor man grew tired of having a neck like that, so he bought a collar made of wax. He put on the collar, then he could not move his head at all. He just looked straight ahead. He did not like that, because he could not turn his head and his eyes could not look at everything. One day, while he walked down the road in the bright sunshine, his wax collar started to melt. Soon the heat of the sun had melted the entire collar. Suddenly, his head dropped down and rested on his chest. *(Children imitate.)* His head rolled around like a wheel. *(Children imitate.)* Remember, he did not have any bones in his neck. Finally, he could see from side to side. He liked that better than wearing a stiff, old wax collar. *(Sit and relax.)*

Stroking. Imagine you are a kitten with soft fur; a kitten that likes to be stroked. Stroke your forehead back and forth with the palm of your hand. Stroke your cheeks with the palms of two hands. Stroke your neck back and forth. Stroke your left arm several times, then your right arm. Try to purr like a kitten.

Things to Imagine

• Imagine you are a cat walking along a fence. Balance yourself so you will not fall off. Taking one step at a time, very slowly, walk across the fence. When you are across, turn around and walk back.

• You are in a meadow. There are two fluttering butterflies. Now more butterflies come. They are every color of the rainbow. Now each butterfly sits on a daisy. The butterflies fold their wings over their heads and rest. Count to yourself. Count to ten. The butterflies fly away toward the sunset. They are gone.

• Pretend you are watching an elf dance on the lawn in front of your house. You watch the elf for a long time. The elf waves good-bye to you and lies under a tree to take a nap.

- Imagine that you are riding on a pony. The pony's mane blows in the wind. Its hoofbeats are very soft. You cannot hear them. You can see the pony and you can see yourself riding along with the wind. The pony stops. You get off its back and find that you are lying on your back here at school.

- Pretend you are a floppy rag doll with no bones. Flop like a rag doll.

- Pretend you are a tree with branches blowing in the wind. Make believe your arms and hands are branches.

- Be a snowperson melting to the ground. Show us how you would do that.

- Be a big block of ice. The sun comes out and you melt slowly.

Think of Pleasant Things. Encourage imaginative thinking by describing pleasant things for the children to visualize. Their eyes should be closed during this exercise. Give the children time to think about each situation.

- Imagine a kite climbing in the wind. It tugs so hard you can hardly hold the string.

- Imagine dew on the grass when sunlight shines on it. It reminds you of diamonds.

- Think of flower beds in the park; changing ripples in water; a birthday cake with yummy frosting and candles; the flickering flames of a campfire; a glass dish of chocolate pudding with whipped cream on top; a friend sitting beside you when you are lonesome; someone to whom you can whisper secrets; a happy birthday party you would like to have; a ride on a merry-go-round; rolling over and over in leaves that make a crunching sound.

- Which of these pleasant imaginings did you enjoy most?

Close Your Eyes. Imagine that you can see things with your eyes closed. Close your eyes now.

- You are in a meadow. What do you see?

- You are at the seashore. What do you see?

- It is a beautiful summer day. Can you see the birds skimming across the sky?

- You are in a bus traveling across the country. Tell what you see.

- Can you see a baby foal or baby calf standing beside its mother? What is happening?

Projected Relaxation

Let Go. Do the actions with the children.

> Let your arms feel heavy.
> Let your legs feel heavy, too.
> Let your hands dangle loosely.
> Let your shoulders droop.
> Let go, and find out how good it feels.
> Let's do that again.

Head and Shoulders. Pretend your head is so heavy, you cannot hold it up. Move your head to the right shoulder; now to the left shoulder. Move your head forward and let it roll slowly from shoulder to shoulder several times. Now roll it around the opposite way and let it drop, ker-plunk, on your chest.

Untying Knots. To help children learn the difference between tension and relaxation, ask them to close their fists tightly, then let go. Pretend their necks, shoulders, thighs, legs, and arms are tied in knots, then pretend to untie them.

> My fist is tied up in a knot;
> So are my arms—all tight.
> My legs have many knots in them,
> They do not feel quite right.
>
> My neck and shoulders are so stiff,
> I can't believe it's true.
> I'm going to undo the knots—
> That's what I'm going to do. *(Relax like a rag doll.)*

Rag Dolls and Wooden People.
The children sit comfortably at their seats or on the floor. One child is chosen to come before the group. The child can choose whether to let her arms hang tense or relaxed. She selects another child to lift up one of her arms. The second child tells whether the lifted arm is tensed or relaxed. If he guesses accurately, then that child may have a turn to be the model.

Poems for Projected Relaxation. These poems help a child feel the difference between tension and relaxation. Have children follow the directions in the poems.

Relax Hands and Toes

Pull your hands in a tight, tight fist.   *(Children follow directions.)*
Pull away each hand and wrist.
Tight, tight, tight, with all your might.
Now, let go!

Tighten your body, hands, chest, feet,
Even your tummy that holds food you eat.
Tight, tight, tight, with all your might.
Now, let go!

Open and Close

Stretch your hands tightly so,   *(Stretch hands, then tighten into fists.)*
Open them and let them go.   *(Open fists and let them drop.)*
Move your wrists up and down.   *(Move wrists.)*
Wiggle like a funny clown.   *(Wiggle whole body.)*
Open hands, close them so,   *(Open and close hands.)*
Open them and let them go.   *(Relax hands.)*
Give your hands a little clap.   *(Clap.)*
Fold and lay them in your lap.   *(Sit relaxed.)*

Stretch

Link your thumbs and stretch your arms high. *(Children follow directions.)*
Up past your ears, up past your eyes.
Pull, pull, and stretch to touch the sky.
Pull—stretch, pull—stretch,
Pull, pull, pull.
Put down your arms and sigh.

Tighten and Let Go

Clench your toes until they are a little ball. *(Children follow directions.)*
Clench them up until there are no toes at all.
Draw your toes way back and now let go.
Lie quietly, eyes closed, and count each toe.

Breathing Activities

1 Feel Quiet. Rhythmic breathing can be detected in children who are relaxed. A few breathing exercises will help the class to feel a sense of calmness. Ask the children to sit or lie down comfortably. Tell them that you are going to ask them to take in a big breath and as they let it out slowly, say "I . . . feel . . . quiet."

Yawns. Open your mouth. Breathe in some air. Think about yawning. Do this three times and maybe you will yawn.

A Poem for Breathing.
     I take a breath: Ah . . .!
     I take a deeper breath: Ah . . . ah . . .!
     And a very deep breath: Ah . . . ah . . . ah . . .! *(Prolong "ah.")*
     Take a deep breath and say your name,
     As we all play this breathing game.
     Take a deep breath. Count slowly to ten.
     And now let's do that all over again.
     Now count backward from ten to one.
     This breathing game is lots of fun!
     In and out, in and out . . . *(Children demonstrate.)*
     That's what breathing is all about.
     Breathing's important! That's understood,
     And oh, it makes us feel so good.

Body Control Activities

Statues. Test for motor control by playing "Statues." The children move quickly around the room. When you say, "Statues," they freeze. If a child moves, he or she sits. The last child left "in" is the winner.

On the Moon. Children walk around the room in different directions, being careful not to touch one another. Ask them to imagine they are on the moon. Their bodies are light and they must move in slow motion with floating steps.

Rocking Head. Children follow movements suggested.

> My head moves to the left and right.
> Rock, rock, rock.
> Ever so smoothly, ever so slowly.
> Rock, rock, rock.
>
> My head moves back and I lower my chin.
> Rock, rock, rock.
> Ever so smoothly, ever so slowly,
> Rock, rock, rock.

I Am on the Ceiling. The children lie on their backs and lift their feet, moving them in slow motion and pretending they are walking on the ceiling. This rhyme may help dispel a fear of heights.

I am a little fly walking on the ceiling. *(Children lift their feet.)*
I walk very softly.
I walk quietly.
On the ceiling, I am upside down.
Walking, walking, walking. Then I stop.
On the ceiling, I am feeling tired,
So I walk across the ceiling and down the side of the wall. *(Lower feet gradually.)*
I never fall at all,
Because my feet stick to the ceiling and wall.
Now my feet are on the floor,
Finally, my feet and I are resting.

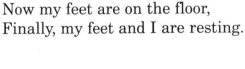

Activities for Feelings

What Do Feelings Look Like? Have the children project their feelings into facial expressions, and have them draw faces showing these expressions. Invite the children to verbalize some of their disappointments, happy moments, sadness, and anger. Follow these discussions with a resting period as you talk about quiet things that will bring feelings of quiet. Display the children's pictures on the bulletin board. Use the poem below to accompany the mood pictures.

- Imagine you are very happy because someone gave you a birthday present. Show feelings of happiness on your face. Draw a picture of a happy face.

- Imagine that your favorite teddy bear has been run over by a car. Its arms and legs are gone. Show your feelings of sadness on your face. Draw a picture of a sad face.

- Imagine that someone ate your lunch and you have no way of getting more food. Show feelings of anger on your face. Draw an angry face.

- Imagine that someone promised to take you to the beach. That person could not keep her or his promise. Show feelings of disappointment on your face. Draw a disappointed face.

- Imagine that you are very tired. You cannot keep your eyes open. Show feelings of sleepiness on your face. Draw a sleepy face.

> Here is a person who's happy.
> Here is a person who's sad.
> Here is a person who's sleepy.
> Here is a person who's mad.

Using the Senses

Take a Walk. The children walk around the room and focus on the sights and sounds. When finished, they come back to their seats and tell what they saw and heard. Ask: "What did you hear? What sound did it make? Could you see what was making the sound?"

Look at a Picture. Find a picture of scenery that includes trees, flowers, birds, bushes, blue sky, clouds, etc. Ask the children to tell what they hear, smell, feel, and taste.

What Does It Feel Like?

- Pretend you have turned on warm water and let it trickle over your fingers. It feels so soothing and warm. You would like to feel the water forever, but you must turn off the tap.

- Imagine that you are climbing into bed and are feeling the cool sheets. In summer, they feel so good on your feet and through your pajamas.

- Imagine that someone has given you a dish of pudding. You can choose any flavor you want. It feels slippery going down your throat.

- Let me know by raising a thumb if you want to tell me how these things feel: towel (fuzzy, rough), hairbrush (prickly), ice cube (cold, wet), silk or satin (soft), crackers (crisp).

Velvet Things. Read through this exercise more than once, in sections, so that the children can absorb the ideas. Be sure to allow adequate time for the children to respond verbally.

You are lying on your back and you are thinking of something that feels like velvet, so soft, such a nice feeling on your fingertips. What are you feeling?

- Is it like the feathers of a canary that sings? What color is the canary?

- Is it like the covering of a butterfly's wings? What color is the butterfly?

- Is it like the petals of a rose? What color is the rose? Whisper the color.

- Is it like your puppy's nose? Is it soft? warm? cold?

- Is it like a mouse's (hamster's) fur?

- Is it like clothing you wear? Which clothing?

- Is it like your hair? How does your hair feel?

- Is it like your own face and lips? Feel your face and lips with your fingertips.

- How does velvet feel to you? Tell us.

How Does It Feel? Read very slowly to give the children a chance to respond to this list of nice things to touch. Use only a few items at a time. Have a box filled with scraps of velvet, lace, foil, or other things mentioned in the exercise. This quiet tactile activity will give children an opportunity to share ideas. (You could also make a "feel" book: paste in pieces of fabric, foil, a zipper, sandpaper, and other things for children to feel and discuss.)

- The softness of a bunny's fur. (Which animals have soft fur? I will pass around a piece of fur for you to feel.)

- The floppy feel of tired arms. (Dangle your arms and let your head flop.)

- The warm, wet sand between your toes. (Imagine that you are at the beach. Can you feel sand between your toes? Tell me in a soft voice.)

- The slippery feel of finger paint. (Tell me how finger paint feels. Do you like to feel it? Why?)

- The feel of delicate lace. (Here is a piece of lace for you to feel. Where have you seen lace? I will show you some lacy paper doilies and later you may cut some to make designs.)

- The crinkly feel of aluminum foil. (Here is a piece of foil that you can feel. How is foil used?)

- The rough feel of a piece of bark. (Here is a piece of tree bark. Pass it around and tell me how it feels.)

- The cold feel of the rain and sleet. (Imagine that you are listening to rain on the windowpane. Place your face against the window. Does the window feel cold as the sleet hits against it?)

- The sticky feel of chewing gum. (How does gum feel in your mouth?)

- A person's hand when I'm afraid. (Hold your friend's hand. Why would someone's hand help you feel less afraid?)

- The icy feel of lemonade. (How does lemonade feel as it goes down your throat?)

- The feel of blankets thick and snug. (Do you like blankets? Why?)

- The crispy feel of buttered toast. (How does toast smell? How does it feel inside your mouth? How does toast taste?)

- The warm feel of my grandma's hug. (Who would like a hug? Would you like someone to hug you? Why? *Note:* Some children do not like to be touched, but oblige any child who asks for a hug.)

Lying in the Sand. Have the children imagine they are lying on the beach. Ask: "How does the sun make you feel? warm? cozy?" Now imagine: "Pretend a friend covers you with sand, letting it trickle over you slowly. How does that feel? Let the sand trickle over your body as I tiptoe once around the room."

Taking a Bath. The children imagine they are in a bathtub filled with warm water, with their arms and legs floating. They close their eyes and feel the warmth of the water. Call attention to how the warm water feels to their legs, arms, and body. Use potent adjectives such as luxurious, good, marvelous, soothing, warm, great, or wonderful.

Can You Hear Me? The children sit in a large circle with eyes closed. One child sits in the middle with eyes also closed, holding a toy. At a signal, one of the children creeps up stealthily and takes the toy, returning to his/her own place and putting the toy under a chair. If any child in the group hears a sound, he/she points to where the sound originated, then someone else has a turn.

Time Between Sounds. Ask children to sit quietly or to lie down, close their eyes, and listen for street sounds or sounds outside of their classroom. Say, "Listen for the time between each sound." After a short period for listening, ask: "Was it a long time between sounds? a short time? What were some of the sounds you heard? Did you hear any of them more than once?"

The Magic Whisper. Tell this story: "Once there was a little Halloween goblin who lost her voice on Halloween. All she could do was whisper." Whisper "Happy Halloween" into a child's ear. He or she in turn whispers the same greeting into the next child's ear; this continues until all children have participated. Continue telling the story: "The sun came out and warmed everything and the little goblin's voice came back. She didn't need to whisper anymore. She could talk in a sweet voice just like you and me. What did the little goblin say about Halloween now that she could talk in a pleasant voice without whispering?" The children respond.

Quiet and Noisy. After reading the following poem to the group, ask: "Which quiet times do you enjoy most? Which noisy sounds make you happy? When is it important to have quiet times? noisy times? Name some noisy sounds that do not belong in this room. Where should these noisy sounds be? What are some good sounds we hear at school? at home?"

A rhyme to share:

Quiet Times

I always like my quiet times,
When I can hear a word that rhymes,
When I can hear a story read,
When I can sleep in my soft bed,
When I give water to my plants,
When I can watch the work of ants,
When I can see a butterfly,
When I can hear a lullaby.
I like my quiet times, do you?
But noisy times can be fun, too!

ACTION RHYMES FOR RELAXATION

Words are an effective means of stimulating movement. Children are aware of the parts of their bodies and all the teacher needs to do is associate the body-part word with the movement. Children usually can perform the movements without verbal directions or demonstration.

Movement can activate the imagination, help to express a mood, and release creative energy. Once children have gained confidence in their own movements, they can cooperate with the group.

Five Little Snow People

Five little snow people, five little snow people,
Stood upon the ground.
Every little snow person, every little snow person,
Was so fat and round.

(Teacher holds up five fingers; five children stand in a row.)

The first little snow person, first little snow person,
Said, "I want to stay —"
The sun began a-shining, sun began a-shining,
So she went away. *(Teacher holds up four fingers; first child sinks to floor.)*

The second little snow person, second little snow person,
Looked so neat and trim.
He was very sleepy, he was very sleepy,
That was all of him. *(Teacher holds up three fingers; second child sinks to floor.)*

The third little snow person, third little snow person,
Saw a sled go by.
So she went a-sledding, so she went a-sledding,
And she said, "Good-bye." *(Teacher holds up two fingers; third child sinks to floor.)*

The fourth little snow person, fourth little snow person,
Stood up straight and tall.
His feet were slowly melting, his feet were slowly melting,
And he took a fall. Oh . . . ! *(Teacher holds up one finger; fourth child sinks to floor.)*

The fifth little snow person, fifth little snow person,
Said, "I want a song.
Sing it very quickly, sing it very quickly,
I can't stay too long!"   *(Fifth child sinks to floor.)*

Five little snow people, five little snow people,
Made of ice and snow.
We would like to keep you, we would like to keep you,
Please, oh, please, don't go.

Repeat with five other children.

Feathery Snowflakes

Feathery, feathery snowflakes, *(Raise arms; let them fall gradually, moving fingers.)*
Falling on the lake.
Feathery, feathery snowflakes, *(Repeat action.)*
Like frosting on a cake.

Little Leaf

Little leaf, little leaf, fly, fly, fly!   *(Hold out palm of hand; then wave arms.)*
The cold wind will take you up in the sky.   *(Look toward sky.)*
The cold wind will whirl you around and around.   *(Turn around.)*
And softly, so softly, you'll fall to the ground.   *(Sink quietly to floor.)*

Me

I make my fingers fly, fly, fly;   *(Wiggle fingers.)*
My back is like a straight, straight wall!   *(Sit tall.)*
My legs are strong; I stretch them straight.   *(Stretch legs.)*
My arms come slowly down, down, down.   *(Lower arms gradually.)*
I close my eyes and count to eight;   *(Close eyes.)*
And then I go to Sleepy Town!   *(Children fold hands in lap and keep eyes*
1-2-3-4-5-6-7-8!   *closed until teacher signals otherwise.)*

Yawning

Boys and girls, when you see a picture of someone yawning, don't you want to yawn, too? I do. I am going to yawn and see if you can catch the yawn from me.

At night, when I'm sleepy,
There's something inside,
That makes me yawn, yawn, yawn. *(Yawn.)*

I lie on my pillow,
And when my eyes close,
My yawn is gone, gone, gone. *(Close eyes.)*

Turtle Goes A-Walking

Turtle goes a-walking,
As slowly as can be.   *(Fingers creep along desk.)*
She peeks her head out of her shell,   *(Extend thumb.)*
And blinks her eyes at me.   *(Wiggle thumb.)*
And when she wants to go to bed,
Inside her shell she tucks her head.   *(Hide thumb inside fist.)*
Ask children to describe the way other animals sleep.

Little Seeds

We are little dandelion seeds, lying in a row.   *(Sit and hug knees.)*
We are hidden in the ground, but very soon we'll grow.   *(Sit up gradually.)*
Now we are coming up, up, up, from our bed below.   *(Rise gradually.)*
Watch us very carefully, and you will see us grow.
We have stems to hold us up, and pretty golden heads.
Oh, there are a lot of us in these flower beds.   *(Stand with arms extended.)*
The warm wind blows around us here, we sway left to right.   *(Move left and right.)*
And when the yellow sun shines down, we make a pretty sight.
But when autumn visits us, and all the frosts appear,
We lie down and say good-bye until another year.   *(Sink gradually to floor and hug knees.)*

Teddy Bear

Pretend you are a teddy bear waiting in a store for someone to buy you. How would you sit? What expression would you have on your face? Someone will come along and buy you and take you to your chair.

Little furry teddy bear,
You look so quiet sitting there.
With your brown and shaggy hair,
Resting still upon your chair,
You look so quiet sitting there.

The Brownie Men

Tiptoe, tiptoe,
All through the town.
You can see the Brownie men,
When the sun goes down.

Sliding down a stairway,
Climbing up again,
Tiptoe, tiptoe,
Go the Brownie men.
— *Adapted*
Form a line and tiptoe around the room.

Goldfish Pets

One little goldfish lives in a bowl,   *(Hold up one finger.)*
Two little goldfish eat their food whole.   *(Hold up two fingers.)*
Three little goldfish swim all around.   *(Hold up three fingers.)*
And although they move, they don't make a sound.

Four little goldfish have swishy tails.   *(Hold up four fingers.)*
Five little goldfish have pretty scales.   *(Hold up five fingers.)*
1, 2, 3, 4, 5 little goldfish, tired as can be,
All can rest in their fishbowl sea.   *(Close eyes; put hands in lap.)*
— *Adapted*

Suggest that the children cut fish from yellow construction paper and place them on the flannel board. If the board is slanted slightly backward, the fish will cling. Children may add one fish at a time and count as they do so.
If needed, glue a small piece of felt on the back of each fish.

I'm a Sunflower Tall

I'm a sunflower tall.   *(Stand tall.)*
I know I won't fall.
Now the wind comes along,
And sings me a song.

It moves me left,   *(Lean to left.)*
It moves me right.   *(Lean to right.)*
It moves back and forth,   *(Continue movement.)*
With all of its might.

Down deep in the ground,
My roots are all found,
So I will not fall,
I'm a sunflower tall.   *(Stand tall.)*

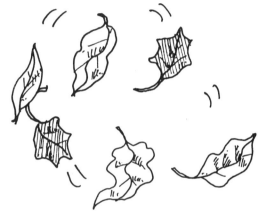

Whirl

Like a leaf or a feather
In windy, cold weather,
We will whirl around,   *(Whirl slowly.)*
Without a sound,
And all sit down together.   *(All sit.)*
—*Author Unknown*

I Am a Robot

I am a robot, big and tall.
Stand me up against the wall.   *(Stand with back to the wall.)*
Wind me, wind me with a key.   *(Make winding motion.)*
Now I'm ready, don't you see?
Walk, walk, stiff and slow.   *(Walk like robots.)*
That is how the robots go.
Walk, walk, in the town.
Oh, I hope I won't run down.
Slow, slow, I'll have to stop.
I've run down and so, ker-plop! *(Sink to floor.)*

The children try to look like robots as they walk. Movements are stiff. Arms make up and down movements. Hands are closed and heads nod up and down. As the robots walk along, heads turn left to right, and when they stop, feet march on the spot.

The Tired Caterpillar

A caterpillar went to sleep one day,
In a cradle bed of silver gray.
She curled up tightly in her nest.   *(Clasp arms across chest.)*
She was tired, so her bed was best.
She slept through winter long and cold,
Tightly in her blanket rolled.

The caterpillar woke one day,
To find that spring was on its way.   *(Unclasp arms and raise to sun.)*
She knew that she had golden wings,   *(Spread arms.)*
No need to crawl on sticks and things,
For now she was a butterfly.
She was so happy she could fly.   *(Pretend to fly.)*

I'll Do These Things

I'll put my hands on top of my head,
And cover my eyes just as you said.
I'll stand up tall and make a bow,
And hide my hands behind me now.

I'll stretch my hands away up high,
Pretend that I can touch the sky.
I'll quickly clap, 1, 2, 3, 4,
Then I'll sit down quietly on the floor.

Perform the actions as indicated. This rhyme can be used when children return from recess.

Counting Daisies

One little daisy is standing in a row.   *(One child stands.)*
Up comes another one, what do you know!   *(Another child stands.)*
Now there are two daisies standing in a row.

Continue the rhyme until all children are standing. Then subtract until all daisies have "blown away," using this version of the rhyme:

Six little daisies are standing in a row.   *(Six children stand.)*
One blows away, what do you know!   *(One child sits down.)*
Now there are five daisies standing in a row.

Children leaving the group return to the rug or floor and relax.

Floppy Freddie

I'll play that I am a magician and with one wave of my magic wand, I will change you from floppy rag dolls into wooden people. Stand like wooden people until I wave my magic wand and change you back into floppy rag dolls.

I'm just like Floppy Freddie,   *(Stand.)*
My doll that's made of rags.
My arms go flop, my feet go flop,   *(Perform actions.)*
My head just wigs and wags.

Now I am like a wooden man,
Who stands up stiff and tall.
My arms and legs are wooden pegs,
I can't bend them at all.
But when I flop my arms and legs,
My body can't be wood,
Because I'm all relaxed,
And, oh, that makes me feel so good.   *(Sit.)*

This Brown Hen

This brown hen doesn't like the rain.   (Point to second finger.)
She shakes her feathers to get dry again.   (Shake hands vigorously.)
This brown hen thinks that it's fun,   (Point to third finger.)
To chase a doodlebug in the warm sun.   (Move fingers around and around.)
This brown hen always likes to rest.   (Point to fourth finger.)
She makes her home in a nice cozy nest.   (Place three fingers inside palm of
                                                other hand.)

Scarecrow Ann

I am funny old Scarecrow Ann.
I flip and I flop as a scarecrow can.
I move my arms, I move my wrists,
I move my legs, and I shake my fists.
I bend away down, I bend away back.
I jump up and down like a jumping jack.
I scare a crow back to its nest,
And then I sit right down to rest.

Perform actions as indicated. Children may play "Scarecrow and Crow." One child is a scarecrow standing stiff and tall. Along flies a "crow." The scarecrow moves and the crow flies away.

Sleepy Kitten

The kitten stretches,   (Stretch.)
Until she is long.
She sings a soft little purring song. (Relax.)
She yawns a big yawn,   (Yawn.)
And stretches some more,   (Stretch.)
And then falls fast asleep on the floor. (Close eyes.)

Summer Morning

It's not dark anymore,
For I see a small light.   (Move fingers rapidly.)
It gets brighter and brighter,   (Move hands apart.)
And away goes the night.

Slowly the sunshine,   (Make circle with arms.)
Lights up the sky.
Two birds begin singing,   (Hold up two fingers.)
In trees nearby.

Three flowers start blooming,   (Hold up three fingers.)
And turn to the sun.
All children know,   (Stand.)
A new day has begun.

Then the sun fades,   (Say quietly and slowly.)
It has been a long day.   (Put hands at sides.)
So now I am tired,
I can no longer play.   (Sink slowly to floor.)

The sun is sinking,
Away in the west,
And so it is time,
To sleep and to rest.

This poem can help children learn the difference between action and relaxation.

Raggedy Ann

Raggedy Ann is my best friend.   (Stand.)
She is so relaxed; just see her bend,
First at the waist, and then at the knee.   (Bend.)
Her arms are swinging, oh, so free!   (Swing arms.)

Her head rolls around like a rubber ball.   (Move head in circular motion.)
She hasn't any bones at all.
Raggedy Ann is stuffed with rags.
That's why her body wigs and wags.   (Move bodies.)

—Louise Binder Scott and J. J. Thompson, *Talking Time.* Copyright owned by author.

Butterfly

I am a butterfly,   *(Move arms slowly up and down.)*
Up in the sky.
The wind blows me softly,
To left and to right.   *(Move body left and right.)*
When the sun goes down,
I sleep all night.   *(Clasp hands above head.)*
When morning comes,
I wake up with the sun.
Being a butterfly is such fun!   *(Pretend to fly.)*

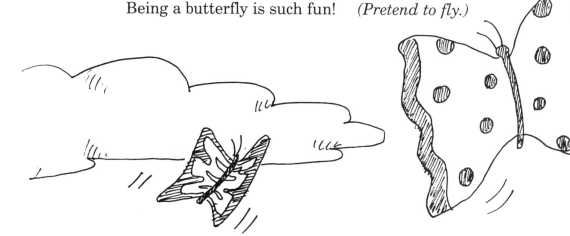

The Clown with No Bones

There once was a clown named Timothy Tones,
And—would you believe it—he had no bones!
From top to toe, no bones at all,
And his head rolled around like a rubber ball.
He wibbled and wobbled when he walked,
And he talked very slowly when he talked.
When he yawned, his mouth was oh, so wide,
That twenty pebbles could hide inside.
And when his shoulders began to sag,
He looked like a great big empty bag!
His arms would dangle, his chin would drop,
And his long legs would flippety-flop.
Timothy Tones went walking one day,
And the sun was so hot, he just melted away.

The first time the children should just listen to the poem. Read it a second time, and have the children stand and demonstrate the actions, heads rolling around, yawning, shoulders sagging, etc. As the clown melts, the children sink to the floor.

—Louise Binder Scott. "The Clown with No Bones," *The Instructor,* June, 1959.

A Relaxed Rag Doll

I brought a visitor to see you today. His name is Sleepy Sam. See how sleepy and lazy he is. He hasn't even dressed to come to school—his hair is all tangled and he never opens his eyes. However, I like him because he is so limp. He cannot hold his arms up as we do. If I hold up his arms and then let go of them, they just fall back where they were. He can bend his arms this way and that way and can fling his body all around, because he is made of rags—he's a limp rag doll. Can you do some of the things he does? With your arms hanging limply at your sides, let your head fall down on your chest; then lift it and let it fall back slowly. Roll your head over on one shoulder, then the other, and now around as if you didn't have any bones in your neck. Let your head drop down lazily, listen to my story, and see if you can do everything it says.

I'm a relaxed rag doll,	*(Stand.)*
I'm as limp as limp can be.	*(Relax head, shoulders, and arms.)*
I cannot stand up straight,	
As you can plainly see.	
I cannot hold my head up.	*(Flop head.)*
I cannot even see.	*(Close eyes.)*
I'm a relaxed rag doll,	
I'm as limp as limp can be.	
Now I will count: 1, 2, 3, 4,	
And I will sit down on the floor.	*(Sink down to floor.)*

QUIET POEMS

Read these poems as the children sit or lie in relaxed positions. As their listening abilities increase, quiet feelings will result when the poems are presented. The poems can also be taped and played as the children are painting, browsing through books, etc.

Quiet Feelings

When quiet feelings come to me,
I sit as still as still can be.
I think about trees or a pretty tune,
Or storybook time, or a big, full moon.
I think about darkness covering the town,
Or twinkling stars as I'm lying down.
I think about wings on a butterfly,
Or clouds moving gently across the sky.
I think about leaves, or a nest in a tree,
And all of these bring quiet feelings to me.

Read slowly and quietly. Pause occasionally to allow children to assimilate feelings and imagery. At the end, ask children to close their eyes and describe what they are thinking.

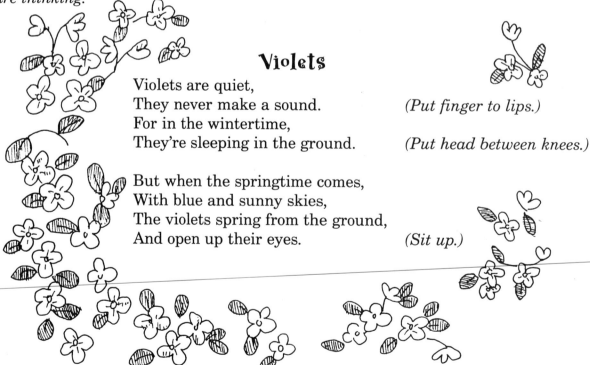

Violets

Violets are quiet,
They never make a sound.   *(Put finger to lips.)*
For in the wintertime,
They're sleeping in the ground.   *(Put head between knees.)*

But when the springtime comes,
With blue and sunny skies,
The violets spring from the ground,
And open up their eyes.   *(Sit up.)*

My Toes

On each of my feet,   *(Point to feet.)*
I have one big toe.   *(Hold up one finger.)*
What can it do,
And where can it go?
It can go with my foot,
To make five toes.   *(Hold up five fingers.)*
But I have just one mouth,   *(Point to mouth.)*
And I have just one nose.   *(Point to nose.)*
I have two big toes,   *(Hold up one finger on each hand.)*
As everyone knows.

Imagine your toes are walking in sand.   *(Pause for imagery to develop.)*
The sand is warm and it feels so grand.
Imagine your toes are walking in mud.
They pull and they slip with a soft, squishing thud. *(Pause.)*
Now imagine your toes are on a soft rug.
Sink deep inside and pretend you're a bug,
Hiding inside that lovely soft rug.   *(Pause.)*

Children lie on the floor. Ask, "Can you move your great big toes as easily as you move your nose?"

Nap Time

It is always best,
To take a rest.
Take out your little key,
Lock up the door,   *(Turn fingers as if turning a key.)*
Pull down the shades,   *(Pretend to pull down eyelids.)*
And then you cannot see. *(Close eyes.)*

Pets' Dreams

There is a land where pets all go,
To have a little nap.
It is a very sleepy land,
We can't find on the map.

A kitten dreams of tiny mice,
She cannot catch a one.
She dreams of bowls all filled with cream,
And that is lots more fun.

A pony dreams of meadows,
Where the grass is sweet to eat.
Where he can gallop, trot, and run,
And exercise his feet.

A teeny, tiny velvet mouse,
Will take a nap with ease,
Away from teasing pussycats,
She dreams of cakes and cheese.

After you have read the poem, ask individuals to tell about their pets' dreams and their own dreams. Say, "Close your eyes and dream a lovely dream. Tell us about it."

Quiet Things

Quiet things are peaceful,
They are nice to have around.
Autumn leaves are floating,
Gently to the ground.

A cat is moving softly,
With feet so velvet light.
Gold butterflies all fluttering,
When the day is bright.

Feathery, tiny snowflakes,
Make a snowy mound.
Don't you like the quiet things,
That make a lovely sound?

Say, "What quiet things do you like? If everything in this room were noisy all of the time, how would you feel about that? Why?

The Ocean

I lie on the sand and listen,
To the ocean all day long.
The ocean makes a swishing sound,
And I listen to its song.
Swish, swish, swish,
Swish, swish, swish.

I lie on the sand and listen,
To the ocean's lullaby.
Even the fish like the swish,
As the ocean waves roll by.
Swish, swish, swish,
Swish, swish, swish.

Children say "swish, swish, swish" with the teacher, prolonging the "sh" sound to simulate the sound of the ocean.

Imaginings of Summer

I'm lying flat upon the ground,
In clover growing sweet and clean.
A small gray bug crawls up a stem,
Some other bugs crawl in between.

The blades of grass must seem like trees;
Each brave bug wonders as she goes,
"Is this a planet or a plane?"
And one bug rests upon my nose.

The sky is clear and sparkling blue,
With clouds like scoops of pink ice cream,
I feel so "comfy" and relaxed,
I like to watch the bugs and dream.

Say: "Could you imagine yourself in a field of sweet-smelling clover? Can you see the bugs? How does a blade of grass seem to a bug? Have you ever seen pictures in the clouds? How did the poem make you feel? If you can read, perhaps you would like a copy of the poem to take home to read to your family. We can learn the poem, say it together, and tape it."

The Little Yellow Duckling

The little yellow duckling is taking his nap,
    (Sh . . . everybody, just whisper, don't talk.)
He's worked all day and he needs his rest.
    (Sh . . . everybody, just tiptoe, don't walk.)

The little yellow duckling was down by the pool,
Watching the minnows swim,
And up by the beehive on top of the hill,
Which was a long way for him.

And down by the brook, where the thirsty cows,
Come to drink and wade,
And nibble the grasses along the edge,
And rest in the willow's shade.

So the little yellow duck has been busy today,
    (Sh . . . everybody, just whisper, don't talk.)
He's all tired out and he needs his rest.
    (Sh . . . everybody, just tiptoe, don't walk.)

— *Author Unknown*

Children say the lines in parentheses, softly and slowly. Ask the children, "How did the poem make you feel?"

What I Would Like to Be

I would like to be a cloud,
    A fluffy cloud, a puffy cloud,
A cottony, soft, and downy cloud,
    Floating up in heaven.

With not a thing to do all day,
    Except to dream, except to play;
A sleepy cloud that floats away,
    Every day in seven.

Say, "Wouldn't it be fun to be a cloud? Imagine that you are a cloud floating around the room. Tiptoe and float. When you are tired of floating come back to the rug and tell about your experience."

Think of Water

Let's think of water:
Water is a lovely thing—
Bright and rippling in a spring,
Dark and quiet in a pool.
In a gutter, brown and cool.
In a raindrop, silver gray,
In a river, ripples play,
In a pitcher, frosty cold,
In a bubble, pink and gold,
In a rainbow after rain,
And droplets on a windowpane.
Water swishing in the sink,
When I go to get a drink.
Water is a lovely thing,
Water makes me want to sing.

You may wish to record this poem for a quiet time. Suggest that children add their own water experiences or thoughts. Make a list of their images on a chart.

Lazy Time

In summer, when the sun in warm,
And skies are very blue,
I like to lie down in the grass,
With not a thing to do.

The tall green trees reach up so far,
They nearly touch the sky.
Imagine clouds are shaped like sails,
As they go drifting by.

I wish I were just tall enough,
To pick a cloud today,
And ride on it to far-off lands,
Where all of us can play.

When I lie here and close my eyes,
I wish that there would be,
Just nothing in this whole wide world,
But sky, trees, clouds, and ME!

Read this poem slowly to the children as they lie in comfortable positions. Observe members of the group and note which ones appear to be relaxed. Ask: "Where would you go if you were riding on a cloud? Do you ever like to be by yourself? Close your eyes and think about a place to go. Tell about it. If you could catch a cloud, what would you do with it?"

SONGS

I Am Special

(Tune: "Frère Jacques")

Verse 1:

I am special,
I am special.

Yes, I am,
Yes, I am.

I am **very** special,
I am **very** special.
Yes, I am,
Yes, I am.

—*Jim Powell*

Verse 2:

You are special, *(Touch a friend!)*
You are special.

Yes, you are,
Yes, you are.

You are **very** special,
You are **very** special.
Yes, you are,
Yes, you are.

It's Me!

(Tune: "It's Me, It's Me, O Lord")

It's me,
It's me,
It's me, my friend,
Standing in the farmer's yard.
(Repeat chorus.)

It's me,
It's me,
It's me my friend,
   Standing in the farmer's yard.
(Repeat.)

It's not the dog, not the cat, but
It's me, my friend,
Standing in the farmer's yard.
(Repeat verse.)

It's not the horse, not the cow, but
It's me, my friend,
Standing in the farmer's yard.
(Repeat.)
*Use other animals for verses: goat,
lamb, chicken, turkey, goose, pig, etc.*

Final verse:
It's me,
It's me,
It's me, my friend,
Standing in the farmer's yard. *(Repeat.)*
—*Jim Powell*

REFERENCES

Armstrong, T. (1994). *Multiple Intelligences in the Classroom.* Virginia: Association for Supervision & Curriculum Development (ASCD).

Bellanca, J., Chapman, C., and Swartz, E. (1994). *Multiple Assessments for Multiple Intelligences.* Illinois: IRI/Skylight.

Cherry, C., Godwin, D, and Staples, J. (1989). *Is the Left Brain Always Right? A Guide to Whole Child Development.* California: Lake.

Educational Leadership 55, No. 1 (September, 1997). "Teaching for Multiple Intelligences." Virginia: Association of Supervision & Curriculum Development.

Gardner. H. (1993). *Frames of Mind: The Theory of Multiple Intelligences.* Tenth Anniversary Edition. New York: Basic Books.

Gardner, H. (1993). *Multiple Intelligences: The Theory in Practice: A Reader.* New York: Basic Books.

Goleman, D. (1995). *Emotional Intelligence: Why it can matter more than IQ.* New York: Bantam Books.

The New City School (1994). *Celebrating Multiple Intelligences: Teaching for Success.* St. Louis: The New City School, Inc.

The New City School (1996). *Succeeding with Multiple Intelligences: Teaching Through the Personal Intelligences.* St. Louis: The New City School, Inc.

Shore, R. (1997). *Rethinking the Brain: New Insights into Early Development.* New York: Families and Work Institute.

Teele, S. (1992). *Teele Inventory of Multiple Intelligences (TIMI).* Riverside: University of California.

Teele, S. (1995). *The Multiple Intelligences School: A Place for All Students to Succeed.* California: Citrograph Printing.